Seymour Simon

PLANET MARS

chronicle books · san francisco

To my grandson Joel (teenage years, here he comes) from Grandpa (I remember them well)

The author especially thanks David Reuther and Ellen Friedman for their thoughtful editorial and design suggestions as well as their enthusiasm for the SeeMore Readers. Also many thanks to Victoria Rock, Beth Weber, Molly Glover, Tracy Johnson, and Nancy Tran at Chronicle Books for their generous assistance and support of these books.

Mercury

Venus

Permission to use the following photographs is gratefully acknowledged:

Front cover, back cover, pages 6–7, 14–15, 29: © ESA; page 1: © NASA and the Hubble Heritage Team; pages 2–3, 8–9, 16–17, 18–19, 22–23: © NASA/JPL; pages 4–5: © NASA/Science Source; pages 10–11, 30–31: © NASA/JPL/Malin Space Science Systems/MGS; pages 12–13, 28: © NASA/JPL/Viking Project; pages 20–21: © NASA/JPL/IMP Team; pages 24–25: © NASA/JPL/Cornell/Jason Soderblom and Jim Bell; page 26: © NASA/Photo Researchers, Inc.; page 32: © NASA/JPL/Cornell.

Book design by E. Friedman.
Typeset in 22-point ITC Century Book.
Manufactured in China.

Library of Congress Cataloging-in-Publication Data
Simon, Seymour.
Planet Mars / Seymour Simon.
p. cm. — (Seemore readers)
ISBN-13: 978-0-8118-5404-7 (library edition)
ISBN-10: 0-8118-5404-3 (library edition)
ISBN-13: 978-0-8118-5405-4 (pbk.)
ISBN-10: 0-8118-5405-1 (pbk.)
1. Mars (Planet)—Juvenile literature. I. Title.
QB641.S4947 2006
523.43—dc22
2005010108

Distributed in Canada by Raincoast Books
9050 Shaughnessy Street, Vancouver, British Columbia V6P 6E5

10 9 8 7 6 5 4 3 2 1

Chronicle Books LLC
85 Second Street, San Francisco, California 94105

www.chroniclekids.com

Mars is the fourth planet from the Sun.

Mars is closer to Earth than any other planet except Venus.

Mars is 140 million miles from the Sun.

Mars is a small planet. If Earth were hollow, seven planets as big as Mars could fit inside.

Mars takes about 687 Earth days to travel around the Sun. That means that one Martian year is almost twice as long as a year on Earth.

Mars is an orange-red planet.

The early Romans thought the color

looked like blood.

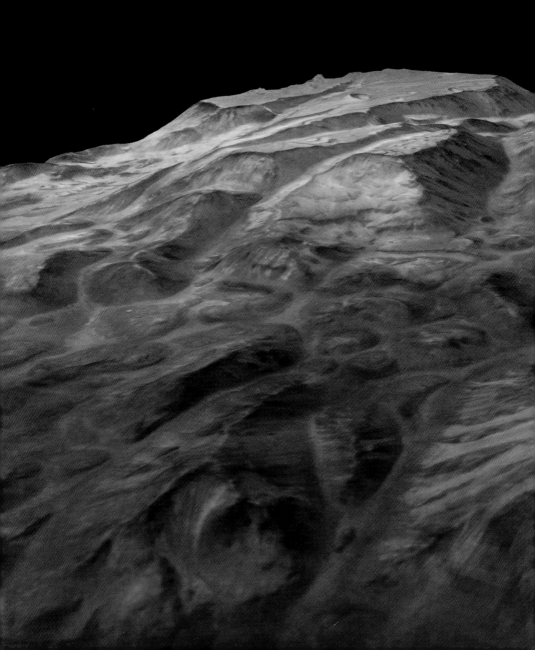

They named the planet Mars after their god of war.

Now we know that the red color is because of rust in the soil of Mars.

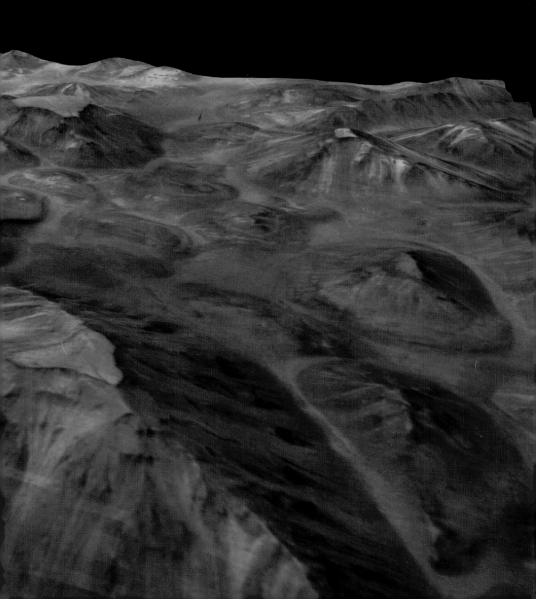

Long ago, some people
looked at Mars through
telescopes and thought
that its surface was
covered by canals dug
by Martians.
Now that we've visited
Mars, we know that
there are no canals
and no Martians.
We have not found any
life at all on Mars.

Mars has polar caps made of ice. But the amount of water left on Mars is tiny compared to the water on Earth. There are no lakes or rivers on Mars.

All the water is in polar ice caps, like the one pictured here, or buried beneath the surface of the planet.

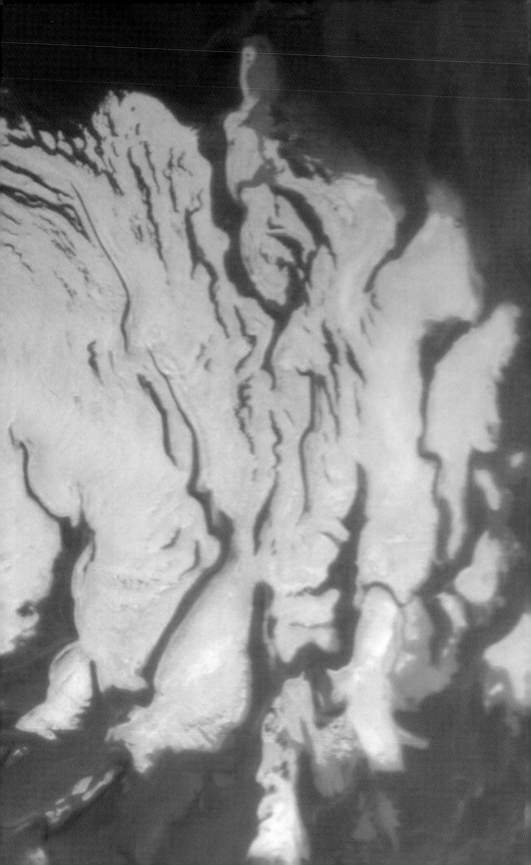

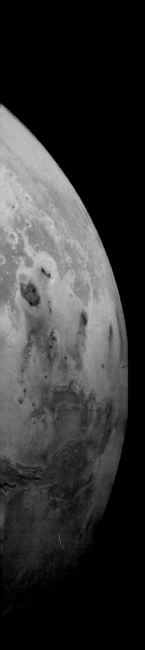

The surface of Mars
has craters, mountains,
valleys, and plains.
The red arrow points
to the biggest valley
on Mars.
It is called the Valles
Marineris (VAILS MARE-
in-AIR-es). It stretches
nearly 3,000 miles.
That is ten times longer
and four times deeper
than our Grand Canyon.

Mars was once a very hot planet with volcanoes just like Earth has.

The biggest volcanic peak on Mars is called Olympus Mons (o-LIMP-us MONS). It is 15 miles high.

That is three times higher than Mount Everest, the tallest mountain on Earth.

On July 4, 1997, the Pathfinder (Path-FIND-er) spaceship landed on Mars.

Pathfinder touched down on a field of rocks and boulders. The two hills in the distance are each about 100 feet high.

Pathfinder carried a small robot vehicle named Sojourner (SO-jurn-er). Sojourner was about the size of a toy wagon and weighed 23 pounds. It took pictures and did experiments with Martian soil. Moving at only 2 feet per minute, it traveled 328 feet in 83 days.

Pathfinder and Sojourner took 16,000 photographs.

They also measured the winds and weather on Mars.

Because of these experiments, scientists think Mars once had lakes and streams.

The rounded rocks and pebbles on this field may have been left behind by floods that once covered Mars.

In January 2004, two rovers named Spirit and Opportunity (OP-or-TUNE-ity) landed on opposite sides of Mars. The Spirit rover traveled over 2 miles to study rocks in the Columbia Hills.

You can see the tracks
Opportunity left on the red
soil of Eagle Crater.
Opportunity found that the
rocks in this crater were
once covered by water.

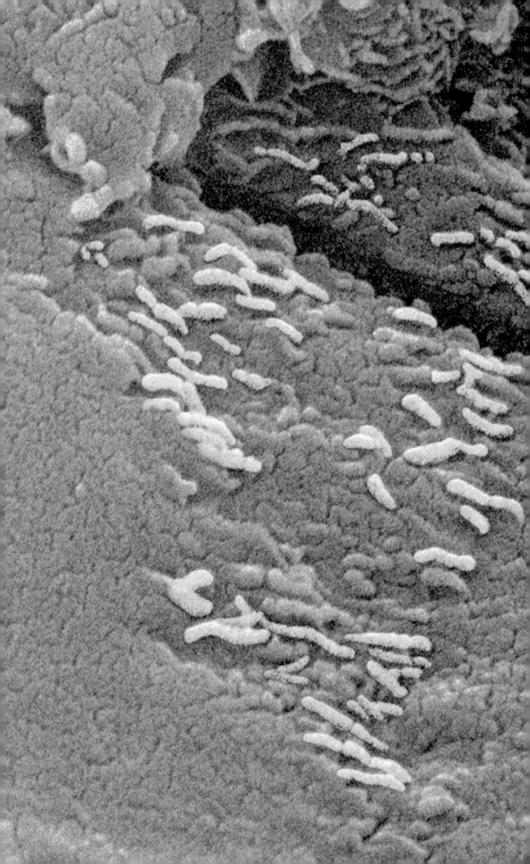

This is a greatly enlarged photo of very tiny objects found inside a meteorite (MEAT-e-or-ite) that came from Mars.

A meteorite is a rock from somewhere in space that lands on the surface of Earth.

The largest object shown here is less than 1/100 the width of a human hair.

Some scientists think that these objects are fossils of bacteria that lived on Mars more than 3.6 billion years ago.

Mars has two small moons that look very bright in the Martian sky. Phobos (FOE-bose) is 17 miles long and 12 miles wide. Deimos (DIE-mose) is 9 miles long and 7 miles wide.

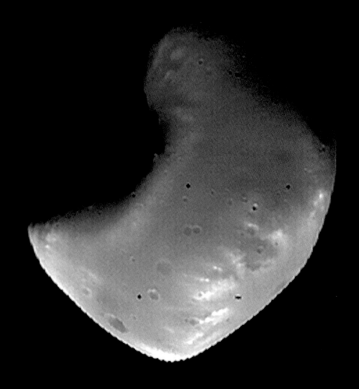

Phobos races around Mars three times in a single day.

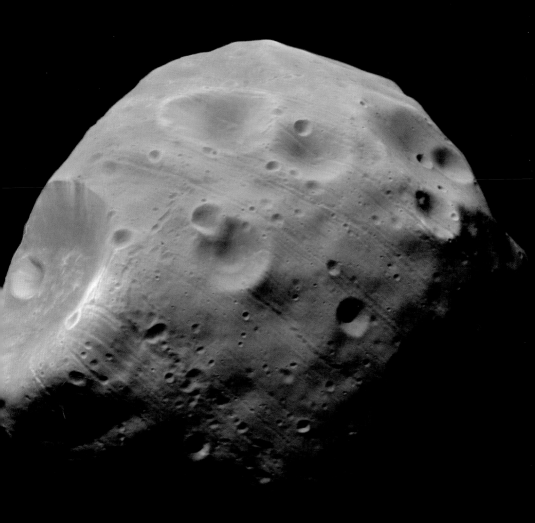

At one time in the past, Mars had more water and was much like Earth.

How did Mars become such a dry planet? And was there ever life on Mars?

In the future, we will send more rovers and perhaps human explorers to try to answer these questions.

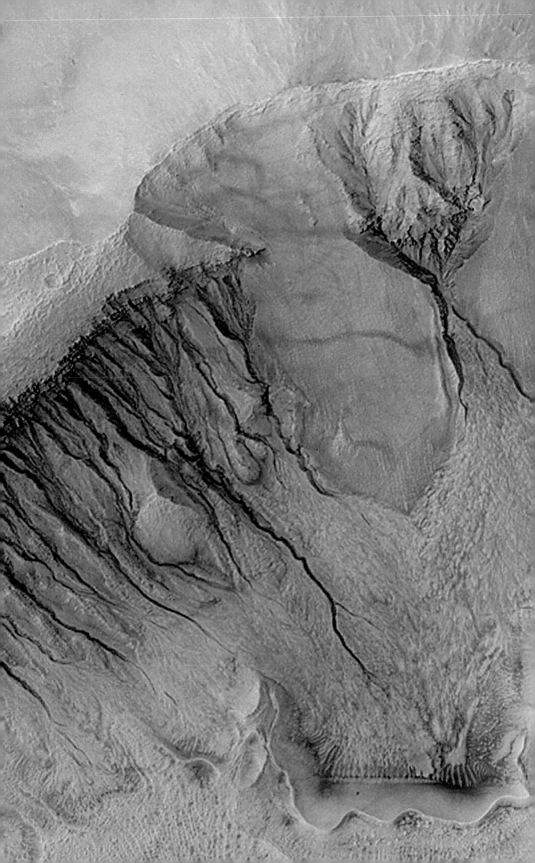

At one time, people were afraid that Mars was the home of aliens.

Today, it is exciting to think that Mars may once have been the home of life beyond Earth.

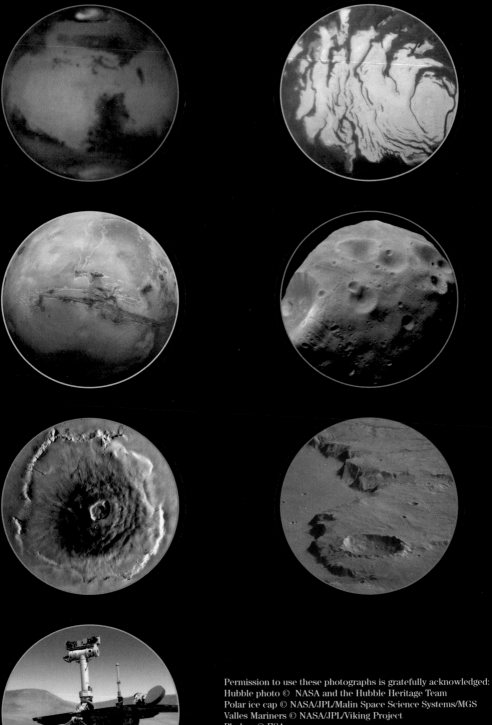

PLANET MARS

SEYMOUR SIMON

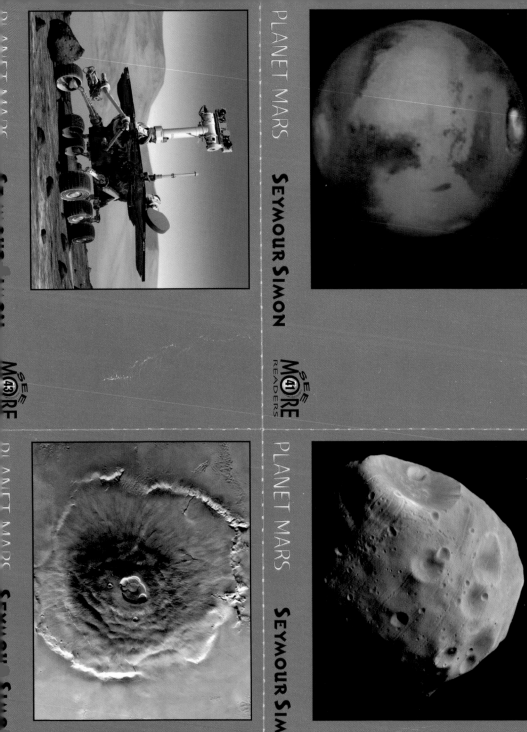

PLANET MARS

SEYMOUR SIMON

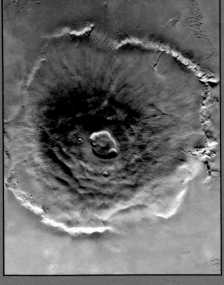

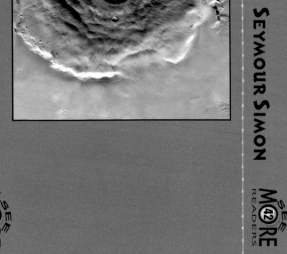

PLANET MARS

SEYMOUR SIMON

Planet Mars

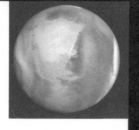

Mars is the fourth planet from the Sun.
It is a cold, dry planet with
no liquid water on the surface.
The red color is because
of rust in the soil.

Published by Chronicle Books LLC
Photograph © NASA and the Hubble Heritage Team

Spirit Rover

The Spirit rover is a small robot vehicle
exploring Mars. It takes pictures and
makes other kinds of measurements
on the surface of Mars.
It can travel about
300 feet in a day.

Published by Chronicle Books LLC
Photograph © NASA IPL

Phobos Moon

Phobos is the larger of Mars's two moons.
It is about 17 miles long and 12 miles wide.
It races around Mars three
times in a single day.

Published by Chronicle Books LLC
Photograph © ESA

Olympus Mons Volcano

Olympus Mons is the biggest volcanic
peak on Mars. It is 15 miles high, three
times taller than the tallest mountain
on Earth. Volcanoes on Mars are
no longer active.

Published by Chronicle Books LLC
Photograph © ESA